CYBER PHONE

BY RICHARD TAYLOR

ILLUSTRATED BY PULSAR STUDIO

First Flight

Titles in More First Flight

Comic Chaos	Jonny Zucker
Into The Deep	Jonny Zucker
Cyber Phone	Richard Taylor
Mutt	Jane A C West
Captured!	Alison Hawes
Robot Goalie	Roger Hurn
Alien Eggs	Danny Pearson
Just in Time	Jane A C West
The Speed Flyers	Jonny Zucker
Super Teacher	Stan Cullimore

Badger Publishing Limited
Suite G08, Business & Technology Centre
Bessemer Drive, Stevenage, Hertfordshire SG1 2DX
Telephone: 01438 791037   Fax: 01438 791036
www.badger-publishing.co.uk

Cyber Phone   ISBN 978-1-84926-450-1

Text © Richard Taylor 2011
Complete work © Badger Publishing Limited 2011

All rights reserved. No part of this publication may be reproduced, stored in any form or by any means mechanical, electronic, recording or otherwise without the prior permission of the publisher.

The right of Richard Taylor to be identified as author of this Work has been asserted by him in accordance with the Copyright, Designs and Patents Act 1988.

Badger Publishing would like to thank Jonny Zucker for his help in putting this series together.

Publisher: David Jamieson
Senior Editor: Danny Pearson
Design: Fiona Grant
Illustration: Pulsar Studio

CYBER PHONE

CONTENTS

CHAPTER 1	Hodge Manor	PAGE 5
CHAPTER 2	Phone City	PAGE 12
CHAPTER 3	Time Freeze	PAGE 17
CHAPTER 4	Cyber Ape	PAGE 21
CHAPTER 5	Myroo	PAGE 24
CHAPTER 6	Second Hand Phone	PAGE 28
MOBILE PHONES		PAGE 30
QUESTIONS		PAGE 32

New words:

rich   invisible

expensive   scruffy

oval   metallic

Main characters:

Josh

Harris

Myroo

CHAPTER 1
Hodge Manor

When your phone's no good, your life's no good.

Josh was in a mess. And it was all down to his phone.

His nasty, brick of a phone.

It had started on his first day at his new school - Hodge Manor - a posh, private school.

Not that Josh's family were rich.
That was the problem - they weren't.

He had passed a special test to get in for free.

Josh wanted to go to the same school as his friends. But Mum and Dad thought it would be great for him to go to Hodge Manor.

It was one of the best schools around.

The problem was everyone that went there was rich. Really rich.

He watched them get dropped off in their parents' sports cars.

They had expensive clothes and new tennis rackets. And amazing, super-smart phones.

Josh hoped no one would spot his scruffy, second-hand blazer.

But what really worried him was his mobile phone.

It was about 5 years old and the size of a shoe.

He spent his first day sitting at the back of class, saying nothing. Trying to be invisible.

But on his way out of the gates, he was stopped by Harris, captain of the football team.

"Nice blazer," said Harris. "Sale on at the charity shop?"

Harris and his friends laughed.

"So, tramp, let's see your phone."

"I don't have a phone," lied Josh.

"Rubbish. I can see it in your blazer. It's huge!"

Josh pulled out his phone. He knew what was coming.

The boys' laughter felt like tiny punches in Josh's belly.

"Wow, it's the first phone ever made!" said Harris. He gave Josh a slap on the side of his face.

"We'll see you tomorrow, tramp."

Josh stared at his phone.

He had tried to look happy when his Dad gave it to him.

Some birthday present - a second-hand phone!

He wanted to throw it under a truck.

Chapter 2
Phone City

Josh didn't sleep that night.

He didn't want to go back to Hodge Manor.

He wanted to tell Mum and Dad what happened, but didn't want them to think he didn't like his special present.

Josh set off to school. He wondered what Harris would do to him today.

He passed a phone shop on his way - 'Phone City'.

He stared into the window and saw the high-tech smartphones.

He saw his sad face in the glass.

Then he looked down at the pavement.

It must have been dropped by a customer.

A brand-new smartphone.

But Josh had never seen a smartphone like this one.

It was bright blue and looked like it was made of glass.

He reached down and touched it.

It began to glow. Josh felt a tingle in his arm.

It was amazing.

On the screen he saw a small green face, with dark, oval eyes.

The face looked right at him.

Suddenly, a bus roared past.

It was his bus. He had missed it and was late for school!

He put the phone in his pocket and started to run.

CHAPTER 3
Time Freeze

Josh was 20 minutes late when he got to the gates.

He knew he was in big trouble.

He could see into his classroom.

The lesson had started.

Suddenly, Josh could feel the tingle of the phone in his head.

He pulled it out and looked at the screen.

Below the green face, he saw a small star.

He touched it with his finger.

The word 'APPS' popped up.

Josh touched the word. The phone hummed.

On the screen, the words 'TIME FREEZE' appeared. He touched it.

There was a sound like lightning crackling inside his head.

The world went silent.

Behind him, the cars on the street stopped moving. Frozen.

A little scared, Josh ran into school.

But his whole class were frozen like statues too.

Frozen in time.

Josh panicked. But the phone began to tingle again. The screen read "TIME FREEZE ENDING".

Josh saw his teacher slowly begin to move.

It was like watching a DVD in slow-motion.

Josh quickly sat down.

The whole class started moving.
He had no idea what had happened.

Had the phone really frozen time?

At least no one had noticed he was late!

Chapter 4
Cyber Ape

At lunchtime, Josh was thinking about his strange morning.

He had forgotten about Harris, until he saw him coming towards him with his gang.

The phone began to tingle again.

Josh pulled it out. The APPS sign was glowing. The words CYBER APE flashed up on the screen.

Josh touched it, just as Harris grabbed his shirt.

"Well, who's been robbing from Phone City?" he said.

Harris tried to grab the phone.

But when he touched it, a noise like a gorilla screaming rang out.

The ground shook. Harris fell to the floor.

"What was that?" said Harris. "What's going on?"

"Leave me alone," said Josh. "Unless you want to find out."

Harris started to shake.

He picked himself up and ran.

Chapter 5
Myroo

That afternoon, Josh became the most popular boy in school.

Thanks to CYBER SPEED and CYBER KANGAROO APPS, he broke school records for the 100 metres sprint and long jump.

But Josh was starting to wonder what the phone really was.

And on his way home, it started ringing.

"Hello," Josh answered.

"Greetings," said a deep, metallic voice. "My name is Myroo."

"I'm Josh."

"Greetings Josh. I think you have found my CYBER 3000 Light Phone"

"Yes. I think so," said Josh.

"Well, thank you for keeping it safe. Can I have it back?"

"Er, yes, of course," said Josh.

"Thank you. Please put it back where you found it. I'll collect it later."

"OK," said Josh. "I'll miss it."

"I'm grateful to you. You are a good Earthling, Josh," said the voice.

Josh sighed. The phone had been fun, but he didn't want to upset Myroo.

She sounded nice, but a little scary...

Chapter 5
Second Hand Phone

The phone was gone, but Josh knew school would get better now.

He passed 'Phone City' the next morning, just to see if Myroo had picked up her phone.

It was gone, but on the ground was a silver box.

There was also a small card.

"DEAR JOSH,

THANKS AGAIN FOR LOOKING
AFTER MY CYBER PHONE.
SORRY I COULDN'T LET YOU KEEP IT.

PLEASE HAVE THIS GIFT, MY OLD
PHONE - A CYBER 2000.
IT ONLY HAS 38 BILLION APPS, BUT IT'S
NOT BAD.
MY FAVOURITE IS 'INVISIBLE'.
I'M SURE YOU'LL ENJOY IT.
BEST WISHES,

MYROO,
QUEEN OF THE RED PLANET"

MOBILE PHONES

- *The first mobile phone that people could buy was brought out in Japan in 1979 by a company called NTT.*

- *By 2009, just 20 years later, about 4.6 billion people living all over the world have a mobile phone contract.*

- *The word telephone comes from two Greek words - "tele" which means "far" and "phone" which means "voice".*

PHONE JOKES

- *What do you call an elephant in a phone box?*
  Stuck.

- *How does a skeleton call his friends?*
  On a telebone.

- *How can you tell if a bee is on the phone?*
  You get a buzzy signal.

QUESTIONS

- *Why is Josh's phone called a 'brick'?*
- *How did Josh win a place at Hodge Manor?*
- *Why did the bullies pick on him?*
- *Where did Josh find the Cyber Phone?*
- *What was the first 'cyber app' he tried out?*
- *What did it do?*
- *Where do you think Myroo came from?*